That's WHAT She SAID

WISE WORDS FROM INFLUENTIAL WOMEN

KIMOTHY JOY

HARPER WAVE

An Imprint of HarperCollins*Publishers*

HarperCollins books may be purchased for educational, business, or sales promotional use. For information, please email the Special Markets Department at SPsales@harpercollins.com.

FIRST EDITION

Designed by Fritz Metsch
All illustrations by Kimothy Joy

Library of Congress Cataloging-in-Publication Data

Joy, Kimothy.
That's what she said : wise words from influential women / Kimothy Joy.
First edition.
p. cm.
ISBN 978-0-06-279676-9
1. Women—Quotations. 2. Women—Illustrations.
HQ1111.J68   2018
305.4—dc23
2017048797

21 22 LSC 13

Dedicated to all the thought-provoking, freethinking, truth-telling women of past and present, beginning with my own fiery mother, Merri Louise Asebedo, who showed me how to blaze a trail of my own

CONTENTS

INTRODUCTION

MY UNDERSTANDING of female power and fortitude began at a very early age.

My mother accomplished much in her lifetime, despite her humble beginnings. She was the eldest of eight children in a Mexican American family and the first and only person in her family to go to college and earn a master's degree. An entrepreneur, schoolteacher, and spiritual leader, she was the breadwinner for a family of six and a pillar of our community. To her last breath at just fifty-five years of age, she was patient and steadfast even in the face of breast cancer—encouraging me to continue to find joy and seize the day. "Go have fun, Kimmy," she told me. Through her, I learned one of my most important lessons: that the strength and resilience of women are limitless.

The 2016 election was a pivotal moment for me. I had already begun to dip my toes into various women's empowerment campaigns through my consulting work, but the election was a wake-up call that it was time to do more. I had been so hopeful that America was ready for its first female president and ready to leverage the power of its female population. But the outcome and overall political climate made me realize that our nation still has a long way to progress.

The election was more than just a political drama playing out—it was about the collective story of women, yet another setback in our striving to gain influence and leadership in our society. I wanted to bring a sincere message of empowerment, respect, and hope for women to a conversation where those elements are often lacking. So I sat down immediately after election day and began to do what I do best: I picked up my paintbrush and painted my feelings.

As I put brush to paper, I wondered what my mother would say to me, were she still alive. I yearned for her advice, her wisdom, and her thoughts on these times. I began to consider what other brave women throughout history would tell me today. How could my generation tap into the women of the past who had risked so much to make their voices heard?

In the weeks and months that followed, I would sit down in my office each morning and begin my day by researching remarkable women throughout history. Poring over biographies and old photographs was a cathartic process that began to reenergize me. I took my time getting to know each of these women, recognizing the context of their lives, the social circumstances they endured, and their meaningful achievements.

I discovered that Marie Curie had once returned to her apartment in Paris to find mobs protesting her love affair, and that Harriet Tubman became a spy for the U.S. Army because she decided she had to do more for abolition. I learned that Amelia Earhart started her own women's fashion line to fund her aviation excursions and that women like Julia Child and Misty Copeland came late to their careers and still found extraordinary success.

I collected stories and wise words from these women and brought them to life on my canvas each day. I painted the portraits with watercolors, then sketched over top of them with black ink pen, using a style I've been experimenting with for years. As I hand-lettered their words on watercolor paper, I knew I had to name the series "That's What She Said"—a cheeky way to reclaim the often crudely sexualized pop culture phrase.

I began sharing these portraits with my small online community. And the members of my community shared the images with their communities. Pretty soon celebrities, major news outlets like the *Huffington Post*, and the leaders of the Women's March on Washington were circulating artwork from this series. My online reach seemed to grow overnight, and soon after there were requests for prints, books, calendars, and even wallpaper.

That's What She Said is meant to be shared and passed along, to help lift up the words of women everywhere. This book has energy and purpose. It is an invitation to consider your own voice on the matters you feel most strongly called to speak on. It is encouragement to build on the incredible work of the women who have come before us.

I selected these women based on the poignancy of their words, their ability to speak their own truths publicly, and the grit and resilience of their stories. They inspired me, and I recognized in all of them a unique way of expressing themselves despite the barriers and challenges they faced.

I'd love for you to join me in honoring the remarkable women of the world. At the end of this book, there is a blank page for you to profile an influential woman from your own life. I encourage you to post these personal profiles on social media under the hashtag #thatswhatshesaid, so that we can all share in one another's stories.

Our words have power. Our stories can change others. And, standing together with the women of the past and present, we can change the world—we can shape the course of *herstory*.

This
IS WHAT
my Soul
IS TELLING ME:
BE peaceful
AND LOVE
EVERYONE.

MaLaLa YousaFzai

(1997–PRESENT)

MALALA YOUSAFZAI began writing undercover for the BBC at the age of eleven, reporting on the atrocities carried out by the Taliban in her own backyard, including her inability to attend school due to her gender. The *New York Times* went on to produce a documentary based on her account of the conditions in Pakistan.

But Yousafzai's rising profile as an activist brought her to the attention of the Taliban, who tried to assassinate her. In a shot heard round the world, the attempted murder sparked international outrage. While Yousafzai remained in critical condition, some two million people signed the Right to Education petition, which led to Pakistan's Right to Free and Compulsory Education Bill.

After recovering from the shooting, Yousafzai and her father founded the Malala Fund to advocate for the importance of girls' education. She won the Nobel Peace Prize in 2014 at seventeen years old and was the youngest person ever to win this honor.

AmeLia EaRHaRt

(1897–1937)

AMELIA EARHART took equality to new heights with her aviation career.

From a young age, Earhart had her eyes to the sky, and she got her pilot's license when she was twenty-seven. She became well known in the piloting world, accepting the opportunity to be the first woman to fly across the Atlantic. Though her role during that flight was minimal, it propelled her to continue breaking records in aviation for women. She became the first woman to fly solo across the North American continent and back, as well as the first woman to fly solo across the Atlantic. And to help fund her expeditions, Earhart became one of the first celebrities to start her own fashion line designed for a variety of women's body types, introducing sensible, functional separates that allowed women to purchase a top in one size and a bottom in another.

Her last flight was during her mission to fly around the world. Though most of the flight was smooth, Earhart and her copilot lost communication with their radio contact on the last leg of their trip. They were never seen again—a mysterious end to an adventurous life.

Women, LIKE MEN, SHOULD try TO DO the IMPOSSIBLE. AND when THEY fail, THEIR FAILURE SHOULD be a CHALLENGE TO others.

Maya Angelou

(1928–2014)

MOST FAMOUS for her memoir *I Know Why the Caged Bird Sings*, Maya Angelou knew how to make the right words soar. An award-winning poet, actress, dancer, writer, and civil rights leader, she made a point not only to speak necessary truths, but to say them in a way that demanded your ear and shot straight to your soul.

At the age of seven, Angelou was sexually abused and did not speak for five years. During that time, she learned to listen and observe, and she read every book she could get her hands on. When she decided to speak again, she had a lot to say—and the rest of her life would be defined by her skills as a writer and orator.

Someone once asked her how she would like to be remembered, to which Angelou responded, "I would like to be known as an intelligent woman, a courageous woman, a loving woman, a woman who teaches by being." Angelou's legacy embodies that statement and is certain to endure.

NeLLie BLY

(1864–1922)

EXTRA! EXTRA! Read all about Nellie Bly, investigative journalist extraordinaire.

Meet Elizabeth Cochran (pen name Nellie Bly). She was a pioneer journalist during the beginning of the twentieth century. Her claim to fame was launching a new kind of investigative journalism—she completely immersed herself in her subject matter in order to get the whole truth, and nothing but.

One of Bly's most legendary investigative journalism pursuits involved faking her own insanity to expose the poor treatment of individuals in asylums, which led to a grand jury investigation into the process of commitment and an increase in funding to improve the conditions of insane asylums. Another legendary pursuit sent her on a record-breaking trip around the world in seventy-two days (à la Jules Verne's *Around the World in Eighty Days*).

Later in life, Bly became an inventor and holder of several patents. She also wrote about the women's suffrage movement, ultimately predicting the year that women would win the right to vote.

Energy RIGHTLY APPLIED and DIRECTED WILL ACCOMPLISH anything.

BiLLie JeaN KiNG

(1943–PRESENT)

THE GAME of tennis met its match when Billie Jean King came on the scene. A former world number one professional tennis player, she's regarded as one of the greatest athletes of all time. With thirty-nine grand slam titles to her name, including twelve singles, sixteen women's doubles, and eleven mixed doubles, it's hard to argue with that reputation.

And while her sports stats are certainly impressive, it's her intangible accomplishments for female equality that make her truly legendary. In 1973, at the age of twenty-nine, King faced off with fifty-five-year-old former Wimbledon champion and outspoken misogynist Bobby Riggs in an epic match coined the "Battle of the Sexes." She, of course, slayed Riggs, and her win was considered a monumental victory for women's tennis. King is also one of the first well-known openly gay athletes and was awarded the Presidential Medal of Freedom for her work advocating on behalf of the LGBTQ+ community.

Simply put, King redefined what it meant to "play like a girl," breaking records and setting new standards the sports world had never seen before.

I WOULD *venture* TO GUESS THAT ANONYMOUS, WHO *wrote* SO MANY POEMS WITHOUT SIGNING *them*, WAS OFTEN A WOMAN.

ViRGiNia WOOLF

(1882–1941)

ACCORDING TO Virginia Woolf, a woman needs two things in order to be intellectually free: money and a room of her own.

Woolf believed that because women were removed from power, they were removed from money—and therefore removed from being creative. Gender pay gap, anyone? Woolf was on to this back in the 1920s.

Woolf's experimentation with stream of consciousness and rich, interwoven interior monologues has made her one of the most notable modernists in the literary world. Her work speaks to the daily obstacles women face due to social inequality—a timeless theme that she addressed with style.

THE PEOPLE must KNOW BEFORE THEY can ACT, AND there IS NO EDUCATOR TO compare WITH THE PRESS.

IDA B. WELLS

(1862–1931)

SILENCE IS GOLDEN, said someone who wasn't Ida B. Wells. One of the early leaders of the civil rights and women's rights movements, she used her dynamic voice on and off paper to bring to light civil issues in order to create positive change.

Wells began her career as a teacher and noticed that a segregated school system created pay discrimination. From there, she went on to become one of the most outspoken writers in investigative journalism for civil rights as well as an active leader of the women's suffrage movement, aiding in the creation of several important women's groups.

These days, you may have seen her image on the 25-cent postage stamp, but Wells's work far transcends any physical accolade, as her refusal to stay silent changed the landscape of civil rights indefinitely.

ANNe FRANK

(1929–1945)

MANY OF US grew up writing in a diary. A place where one's most intimate thoughts, opinions, wishes, and dreams could be safely kept, far from the judgmental eyes of others. But one particular diary has taken on outsize historical significance, providing insight and a touchstone of humanity to the millions who have read it: that of a teenage girl hiding from the Nazis in an attic during World War II.

Anne Frank was just fifteen years old when she died in a concentration camp, after her family's hiding spot in Amsterdam was disclosed to the Gestapo. But her words live on through one of the most famous accounts of the Holocaust ever written. A painfully honest and sincere narrative of her time spent in hiding, Frank wrote poignantly about everything from her fears of being discovered to her dreams about life after the war. For more than seventy years and in over sixty languages, her words have represented one of the most tragic events ever to occur in history—and all the while her belief that people are inherently good still sparks hope.

FRiDa KaHLo

(1907–1954)

YOU MAY know her for her strong brow game, but Frida Kahlo's artistic dedication to individuality and political expression made her so much more than a pretty picture.

Originally intending to study medicine, she began her artistic career while recovering from a nearly fatal bus accident that left her in lifelong pain. She channeled tragedy into internationally acclaimed creativity, as well as peace-driven activism for the Mexican Communist Party.

Kahlo lived as vibrantly as she painted. She treated everyone as an equal and disdained pretension. She danced from relationship to relationship, admitting her overarching sense of loneliness but never losing her dark sense of humor.

Kahlo is one of the most celebrated surrealist artists in the history of ever.

NOTHING IS worth MORE than LAUGHTER. IT IS Strength TO LAUGH and TO ABANDON oneself, TO BE LIGHT.

GRaCe Lee BoGGS

(1915–2015)

MARATHONS ARE completed through a series of small, focused steps. Just as social impact is effected by people working together in small, dynamic groups.

Activist and author Grace Lee Boggs believed that change came not from large revolutions but by unifying passionate, local assemblies to rebuild communities. A tenacious leader, Boggs committed the majority of her life to rebuilding her city of Detroit through a sustainable, intergenerational, multicultural community movement called Detroit Summer. She was also a prominent figure in Detroit's Black Power movement.

Boggs challenged the idea of what it means to be an activist and believed you have to recognize yourself as part of the problem before you can become part of the solution. This mind-set fueled her involvement in every major political movement for eighty years. One step at a time, she lived, worked, and breathed for change until the ripe age of one hundred.

You CANNOT CHANGE ANY Society UNLESS YOU TAKE RESPONSIBILITY FOR IT, UNLESS YOU SEE YOURSELF AS Belonging TO IT, and RESPONSIBLE FOR changing IT.

"HOPE" is the THING WITH feathers — THAT PERCHES in the SOUL — and SINGS THE TUNE WITHOUT the WORDS — AND never STOPS — at all.

EMILY DICKINSON

(1830–1886)

FOR SOMEONE who spent most of her life isolated and in seclusion, Emily Dickinson was a surprisingly worldly writer. Channeling her fear and anxiety of the external world into beautiful rhetoric, she composed nearly eleven hundred poems—observing everything from nature to law, music to politics, fashion to love.

Despite the extent of her writings, no more than a dozen of Dickinson's poems were published while she was alive. She made her sister Lavinia promise to burn her correspondence in the event of her death, but luckily she left no similar instructions for the countless pages of poetry Lavinia found.

Dickinson's first volume of poetry was published four years after her death. Her work has remained in print since that time, and today she is one of America's most well-known and beloved poets. And for someone who was more likely referred to as a "gardener" than a "poet" during her lifetime, well, that's what the literary world might call . . . ironic.

ELLEN DeGeNeReS

(1958–PRESENT)

IT'S HARD to hear Ellen DeGeneres's name and not smile.

The hilarious talk show host has made millions of people laugh since her 1980s debut in stand-up comedy. She landed her big break on *The Tonight Show* with then-host Johnny Carson and began making her rounds on the television talk show circuit, eventually starring in movies and two television sitcoms.

Known to be a terrific dancer, DeGeneres is also recognized for publicly coming out on the *Oprah Winfrey Show* and for being the first openly lesbian actress to play an openly lesbian character on television.

DeGeneres is a humanitarian and a social rights and animal rights advocate. Her combination of humor and courage have made her a prominent role model for the LGBTQ+ community and, frankly, for all.

Of COURSE I am NOT WORRIED about INTIMIDATING MEN.

The TYPE OF MAN who WILL BE INTIMIDATED BY me IS EXACTLY the TYPE of MAN I have NO INTEREST in.

CHiMaMaNDa NGOzi ADicHie

(1977–PRESENT)

CHIMAMANDA NGOZI ADICHIE first learned the word *feminist* in an argument with one of her childhood friends. While she identified with the label, she frequently used qualifiers to make herself appear to be a more "acceptable" version of the stereotypical feminist—at one point referring to herself as a "happy African feminist who does not hate men and who likes lip gloss and who wears high heels for herself but not for men."

Though this was a tongue-in-cheek statement, Adichie uses it to make the valuable point that the word *feminism* is heavy with negative connotation. She has since made it her professional and personal business to change that perception.

Drawing from her global perspective as both a Nigerian and American citizen, the MacArthur Foundation "Genius Grant" winner brings her distinctive voice on feminism and gender to her award-winning short stories, novels, and nonfiction—and most notably with her bestselling book *We Should All Be Feminists*, which presents a unique definition of feminism for the twenty-first century.

IRIS APFEL

(1921–PRESENT)

AGE IS just a number. And Iris Apfel is living proof.

Relatively unknown for most of her life, Apfel didn't achieve national acclaim until she was eighty-three years old. A last-minute cancellation left a spot open in the Metropolitan Museum of Art fall fashion show. The museum curator approached Apfel about showcasing her lifelong personal jewelry and clothing collection. The result? Overnight fame. People loved Apfel's eccentric and innovative combinations, mirrored after her own personal "more is more" style.

Today, Apfel is a fashion icon who shows no intention of slowing down. From starring in her own documentary to being featured in dozens of magazines, she is a fashionable reminder to be your original self and to have fun while doing it.

SOJOURNER TRUTH

(1797–1883)

SOJOURNER TRUTH fought for freedom, equality, and social justice with such perseverance that the legacy of her name rings true with rich symbolism to this day.

Born Isabella Baumfree in upstate New York, Truth escaped slavery in her late twenties and began her journey as an African American abolitionist and women's rights activist. A woman of deep faith, she gave herself the name Sojourner Truth and devoted her life to ending slavery and preaching morality.

Truth became an important leader during the Civil War, traveling the country to share her experiences. She was a talented orator who moved and motivated people with her words. Her impromptu speech "Ain't I a Woman?" is one of the most famous abolitionist addresses of all time.

Truth
IS
POWERFUL
and
IT
Prevails.

GRace HOPPeR

(1906–1992)

A BRILLIANT mathematician and computer scientist, Grace Hopper joined the U.S. Naval Reserve in 1943. She had to get special permission to enlist, weighing in fifteen pounds shy of the navy minimum. Fortunately, they were interested in her brains, not her brawn.

In the navy, Hopper was among the first to program the Mark I computer, a landmark system in computer technology. From there, she moved on to the private industry to develop the first compiler for computer programming languages. She was recalled to active naval duty at age sixty to tackle a problem only she could solve. At the age of seventy-nine, she retired as a rear admiral, nicknamed "Amazing Grace."

Hopper actively mentored women and young people throughout her career, emboldening them to take risks and achieve beyond what was typically expected of them. Her pioneering in computer technology redefined the landscape for the next generation of female computer engineers.

EVERY *moment* IS *an* ORGANIZING OPPORTUNITY, *every* PERSON A POTENTIAL *activist*, EVERY MINUTE A CHANCE *to* CHANGE THE WORLD.

DOLORES HUERTA

(1930–PRESENT)

SI, SE PUEDE. Three small words with infinite potential.

Dolores Huerta grew up in a household of labor activists, an environment that heavily influenced her own passionate beliefs and actions later in life. She started out as a teacher but switched to activism when she was struck by the number of students whose struggling families could not afford to feed and clothe them for school. "I thought I could do more by organizing farm workers than by trying to teach their hungry children," Huerta said.

She cofounded the National Farm Workers Association, which later became United Farm Workers. Their slogan, *"Si, se puede"* (Spanish for "Yes, it is possible" or "Yes, one can"), was coined by Huerta and would later inspire Barack Obama's 2008 campaign slogan, "Yes, we can."

A fierce advocate for workers, immigrants, children, and women, Huerta has been arrested more than twenty times for nonviolent civil disobedience in support of her beliefs.

Never BEND YOUR HEAD. Always HOLD IT HIGH. Look THE WORLD STRAIGHT in the FACE.

HeLeN KeLLeR

(1880–1968)

IT MIGHT have been easy to assume that a girl who became deaf, blind, and mute in early childhood wouldn't have much of a life (especially in the 1880s). But you know what they say about assuming.

By the time she was seven, Helen Keller had invented around sixty hand signs to communicate with her family. But she learned a new way to connect with the world when her teacher, Anne Sullivan, began to spell the names of objects into the palm of her hand (called finger spelling).

To further connect, Keller taught herself to speak by feeling people's mouths while they spoke, then copying the movements. Communicating in her own way, she earned her bachelor of arts degree and became a world-renowned speaker, advocating for the visually impaired, women's rights, labor rights, and people with disabilities, among others.

Keller changed the conversation from "What can this girl do?" to "What *can't* this girl do?"

AUDRE LORDE

(1934–1992)

AUDRE LORDE had a way with words.

A black lesbian cancer survivor, she was a poet who wrote with eloquence and candor about the frustrations of being an outsider in every social group of which she was a member. She wanted to be seen for her differences but not judged for them. Her poetry spanned her outrage at civil and social injustices to the need for intersectionality in feminism in a traditionally patriarchal and heterosexist society.

Her literary work won numerous prizes, including an American Book Award, and there is now an Audre Lorde Award that honors lesbian poets. Before she died, she took the name Gamba Adisa, which means Warrior: She Who Makes Her Meaning Known.

IT IS NOT
our DIFFERENCES
THAT *divide* US.

IT IS *our*
INABILITY TO
RECOGNIZE,

accept,
AND
CELEBRATE
those
DIFFERENCES.

YOKO ONO

(1933–PRESENT)

YOKO ONO may be most famous for lying in bed with her late husband, John Lennon, to promote peace, but that doesn't mean she's been sitting around since. An incredibly bold and established activist and artist long before she met Lennon, she has dedicated herself to spreading awareness for various causes through her conceptual art and has inspired millions for more than fifty years.

Having hailed from an aristocratic Japanese family and trained in classical piano, Ono made her way to the United States for college and eventually moved to Manhattan to pursue her career in art. Her work was on the rise when one particular member of the Beatles took notice, sparking a love affair that captivated the public.

Since the 1960s, Ono has advocated for peace through music, artistic demonstrations, and public protests. Traveling the world, she's used her lifelong creativity and talent to encourage new ideas and spread goodwill—whether it be funding Strawberry Fields in Central Park as a tribute to John Lennon or founding a group called Artists Against Fracking to oppose drilling laws.

We are ALL DREAMERS creating THE NEXT WORLD, THE NEXT BEAUTIFUL world FOR OURSELVES AND FOR our CHILDREN.

Only if WE UNDERSTAND, WILL WE care.

ONLY if WE CARE, WILL WE HELP.

Only IF WE HELP, SHALL all BE SAVED.

JANE GOODALL

(1934–PRESENT)

JANE GOODALL was the child who insisted on sleeping with a handful of earthworms. From an early age, her affinity for animals was obvious. Some would say it began when her father gifted her with a toy chimpanzee named Jubilee when she was just a year old.

Eager to study animals in the wild, Goodall always longed to visit Africa, so when the opportunity came about to visit a family friend's farm in Kenya, she eagerly accepted. Once there, she had a life-changing meeting with Louis Leakey, a famed Kenyan archaeologist and paleontologist who helped Goodall embark on her first solo expedition to study wild chimpanzees in Tanzania. Well, sort of solo. As a twenty-four-year-old young lady, she was required by authorities to have an escort . . . so she decided to summon her mother. From there, Goodall went on to be one of the world's most notable experts on chimpanzees. She has spent more than fifty-five years studying the social and family interactions of primates and making discoveries that have rocked the scientific world.

Along with conducting fascinating research, Jane Goodall is an inspiring voice for endangered species, encouraging others to take action to make the world a better place for the creatures who walk it. Jubilee the toy chimpanzee sits on a chair in her home in England to this very day, a reminder of her life's calling.

I AM BUILDING A *fire*, AND EVERY DAY I TRAIN, I ADD MORE *fuel*. AT JUST THE RIGHT MOMENT, I *Light* THE MATCH.

Mia Hamm

(1972–PRESENT)

SO MUCH more than a pretty face on a cereal box, Mia Hamm is a retired professional soccer player, two-time Olympic gold medalist, and two-time FIFA Women's World Cup champion.

An adept dribbler and thoughtful pacer, Hamm was a strong team player. She could rock any offensive position, although she was best known for her prolific scoring, holding the record for most international goals scored by a man or woman until 2013. You would not want to be the goalie playing against this gold medalist.

Hamm became the most marketable female athlete of her time. She had contracts with Gatorade, Nike, and Pepsi, among others—and, yes, she even appeared on a Wheaties cereal box. Largely considered the best female soccer player in history, Hamm inspired a generation of young female soccer players and helped set the stage for the continued dominance of the U.S. women's national team for years to come.

EMMELINE PANKHURST

(1858–1928)

TO SOME, Emmeline Pankhurst might have seemed a little radical. But when your motto is "whatever it takes," sometimes it takes being radical to get the job done.

The OG suffragette, Pankhurst spent her entire life fighting (sometimes very literally) for women's right to vote in the United Kingdom. As founder of both the Women's Franchise League and the more militant Women's Social and Political Union (WSPU), she, along with her fellow suffragettes, was notorious for her often controversial means of gaining attention. From hunger strikes to arson attempts, there was no demonstration too illicit to raise awareness and rally support for the causes in which Pankhurst and the WSPU believed.

In 1928, thanks to more than seventy years of the suffragettes' efforts (and just weeks after Pankhurst died), women in the UK were granted full voting rights.

Owning WHO WE ARE IS Power.

We've GOT to DARE TO STAND out.

JaNeT MoCK

(1983–PRESENT)

JANET MOCK is on a mission to redefine realness. And she's doing it with an ingenious mix of intellect, compassion, and media savvy.

Mock has written and edited several magazines, published a *New York Times* bestselling book, and hosted her own show *So POPular!*, which examined the social and cultural implications in our American pop culture guilty pleasures.

Mock's work has been informed by her experiences with the pressures to conform to societal expectations. A powerful transgender rights activist, she generously shares her story of being a young person who transitioned in the hopes of reaching those who are struggling. She is brilliant at flipping the script on interviewers, causing them to feel for themselves the bizarre way transgendered people are treated by the media.

She is a symbol of hope that people will continue to break through discrimination to find love and success, and be accepted for who they truly are.

NOTHING IN *Life* IS TO BE FEARED, IT IS *only* TO BE UNDERSTOOD.

MaRie CuRie

(1867–1934)

WHERE WOULD the world be without the brilliant Marie Curie? The woman was an unending well of awesomeness.

Curie's work shook up the scientific establishment. She was a pioneer in the field of radiation research, discovering both radium and polonium, and she pushed back against gender discrimination every step of the way.

Curie attended college *in secret* because women weren't allowed to further their educations in Warsaw, Poland, in the 1880s. She studied physics, chemistry, and math in her spare time and received two master's degrees before going on to work in a lab in France.

France was where the real magic—both scientific and romantic—happened. While making major scientific discoveries on the regular, Curie met her future husband. Her clever hypotheses and innovative methods attracted Pierre Curie away from his work with crystals, and the two teamed up in a synchronistic personal and professional partnership.

They were awarded the Nobel Prize for Physics in 1903, making Curie the first woman to win a Nobel Prize. In 1911, Curie became the first person ever to win a second Nobel Prize, this time in chemistry.

JuLia CHiLD

(1912–2004)

AFTER WORKING at a U.S. intelligence agency during World War II (because she was too tall to enlist in the Women's Army Corps!), Julia Child met her husband, and they traveled to Paris for his job in the foreign service. It was while in France that her palate and spirit were expanded by the delightful and unfamiliar terrain of French cuisine.

At thirty-eight years old, Child attended Le Cordon Bleu in Paris and then studied with several master chefs. From there, she went on to write defining cookbooks about French cuisine for an American audience, including *Mastering the Art of French Cooking*. She also became a television icon, starring in various cooking shows that highlighted her hearty humor, playfulness, and distinctive voice.

Child is credited with bringing approachable French cooking into American homes, and she did so with refreshing authenticity and good cheer. She went on to become the first woman inducted into the Culinary Institute Hall of Fame and remains an inimitable legend in the food world.

Not afraid of the limelight or stepping out of her comfort zone, Child is a reminder to all to live with joyful curiosity regardless of age, and never to be afraid to cook with a whole lot of butter.

The ONLY time to EAT DIET FOOD IS *while* YOU'RE WAITING *for* THE STEAK *to* COOK.

When SOMEONE IS CRUEL OR ACTS LIKE A BULLY, YOU DON'T STOOP to THEIR LEVEL. No, OUR MOTTO IS, WHEN they GO LOW, WE go HIGH.

MiCHeLLe OBaMa

(1964–PRESENT)

FROM AN early age, Michelle Obama was acutely aware that her gender and race were going to play a large role in her life.

As a young woman growing up on the South Side of Chicago, she faced prejudices throughout her education. But she used that to fuel her achievements and obtained degrees from Princeton and Harvard Law—after which she landed a job as an associate at a law firm. It was there she met her future husband, Barack Obama.

Obama would go on to become one of the most beloved First Ladies of all time. As First Lady, she referred to herself as "mom-in-chief," taking on issues of childhood obesity with her "Let's Move!" campaign and openly supporting LGBTQ+ rights. As the first African American First Lady, Obama was under additional scrutiny, but she maintained high popularity thanks to her intelligence, style, and wit.

Speculation still stirs over whether Obama will run for president of the United States herself one day. Whether or not this happens, she will be remembered for the grace and unwavering confidence she exuded during her tenure as First Lady.

CLaRa BaRToN

(1821–1912)

WHILE CLARA BARTON herself may not be a household name, you may have heard of a little organization she started called the American Red Cross.

Barton was compelled to serve others from a young age, and that carried from her early years as a teacher to her compassionate work as a hospital nurse during the Civil War and on to her founding of the American branch of the Red Cross. Though she was severely shy as a child, her time as a teacher helped her develop confidence—so much so that she fought for equal pay then and throughout her professional life.

To call Barton a pioneer of what is now America's modern-day disaster relief would be an incredible understatement. She was a groundbreaking humanitarian—not only for women at a time when very few worked outside their home, but also in laying the building blocks for the future of America's most well-known disaster-relief organization.

I may SOMETIMES BE WILLING TO TEACH FOR nothing, BUT IF PAID AT ALL, I SHALL never DO A MAN'S work FOR LESS THAN A MAN'S pay.

MaRLeNe DieTRicH

(1901–1992)

MARLENE DIETRICH was the original Lady Gaga. Dietrich, a German American performer, was a talented entertainer—an actress, singer, movie star, and fashion icon—until the day she died. Known for her glamorous and androgynous film roles, she publicly defied sexual norms and was openly bisexual.

Dietrich was also an outspoken critic of the Nazi government. She used her fame and fortune to advocate for the Jewish community during World War II. From housing German and French refugees to aiding in their pursuit of American citizenship, Dietrich did everything in her power to help Jewish individuals at a time when they couldn't help themselves.

Some of the humanitarian works she is noted for include being one of the first celebrities to sell war bonds, giving up her entire salary from one of her films ($450,000 in 1937) to help refugees, and working with other German celebrities to create a charity fund to help Jews escape from Germany.

SEX:

IN America
an OBSESSION.

IN other
PARTS OF
the WORLD
A
FACT.

SHiRLeY CHiSHOLM

(1924–2005)

IMAGINE IT'S 1972. You're a black woman. And you're running for president of the United States.

Meet Shirley Chisholm. Before a lot of female political firsts, there was Shirley. The first black woman elected to the U.S. Congress, she ran for president in 1972, despite being criticized and ridiculed by both Republicans and Democrats, as well as by the Black Caucus.

Although she came away with only a small percentage of votes, her efforts influenced her opponent's policies, and she paved the way for more women to run for political office—and, eventually, for president of the United States.

Chisholm's life embodied her belief that "if they don't give you a seat at the table, bring a folding chair."

AT PRESENT, *our* COUNTRY NEEDS *Women's* IDEALISM AND DETERMINATION, PERHAPS *more* IN POLITICS THAN *anywhere* ELSE.

IT'S a SIGN OF *your* OWN WORTH SOMETIMES *if* YOU *are* HATED BY *the* RIGHT PEOPLE.

MiLeS FRaNKLiN

(1879–1954)

IN 1901, Australian author Miles Franklin found early success with her national bestseller, *My Brilliant Career*, which told a refreshingly honest story about a teenage girl growing up in rural Australia. Over a century later, *My Brilliant Career* is still considered an Australian classic.

Her subsequent books sparked so much controversy in their blatant rejection of traditional feminine roles that the sequel wasn't deemed appropriate to publish until 1946.

In addition to becoming a famous author at the age of twenty-one, Franklin was an active feminist who traveled overseas and worked with the women's labor movement in Chicago, and for several feminist and progressive causes in London.

When she returned to Australia to live out the remainder of her days, her final wish was that her estate be used to found the now notable Miles Franklin Award for Australian fiction. She is considered an Australian hero and one of the country's most celebrated female authors.

You CAN START LATE, Look DIFFERENT, BE UNCERTAIN, and STILL Succeed.

MiSTY COPeLaND

(1982–PRESENT)

MISTY COPELAND is a ballet dancer who broke the mold for ballerinas everywhere when she joined the American Ballet Theater (ABT). Though she did not begin to study ballet until the age of thirteen, when she attended her first class at the local Boys & Girls Club, Copeland was considered a prodigy and became one of the youngest soloists ever to be accepted by the ABT. She was also the only black female ballet dancer during her time with the dance company, and the first in the ABT's history to be promoted to principal dancer.

After her delayed onset of puberty at age nineteen, Copeland struggled with her new curves. Her body type no longer matched the idealized expectations of what a ballerina should look like, and this took a toll on her body image and, consequently, her dancing. With her friends' support, she began embracing her shapely figure and dancing with more confidence than ever, thus deconstructing the unrealistic, unhealthy ideals long held by the ballet industry.

Copeland's vast repertoire of performances onstage and on-screen ranges from classics such as *The Nutcracker* and *Swan Lake* to a music video with Prince.

ELeaNOR ROOSeVeLT

(1884–1962)

WITH THESE words, Eleanor Roosevelt voiced her own elegant version of today's maxim "you do you."

A woman of immeasurable kindness, stoicism, and strength, Roosevelt is considered the Mother Teresa of democracy and one of the most vocal women to inhabit the White House. As First Lady, she connected to the public in an unprecedented way, using her personal newspaper column to share her messages of humanitarian advocacy—and, in doing so, became a prolific public figure. Following her husband's death, she continued her public service, accepting an appointment as a delegate to the U.N. General Assembly, and going on to become a key influencer behind the United Nations' Universal Declaration of Human Rights.

Roosevelt lived a life that mirrored her values and was steadfast in using her platform to work toward liberty and justice for everyone.

Mae Jemison

(1956–PRESENT)

YOU CAN grow up to be anything . . . or all the things.

Mae Jemison always knew she wanted to explore. She went to Stanford at the age of sixteen to become a chemical engineer, then attended Cornell University Medical College and worked as a medical officer in the Peace Corps. But she was always bothered by the fact that there were no female astronauts, so she became an astronaut, too. In 1992, Jemison became the first African American woman to travel in space.

Her larger-than-life career and professional pursuits led her to be a strong education advocate for women and minorities in the sciences. Jemison recognized the untapped potential that could be unleashed if more women and minorities were given the opportunity to launch themselves to greater heights.

Never LIMIT yourself BECAUSE of OTHERS' LIMITED imagination; Never LIMIT others BECAUSE OF your OWN LIMITED imagination.

NORA EPHRON

(1941–2012)

EVEN TODAY, it's not easy for women to be accepted as comedic writers and performers by mainstream society.

Much of contemporary female comedy owes a solid to the one and only Nora Ephron, a trailblazing Oscar-nominated screenwriter, essayist, journalist, film director, and playwright. And if you enjoy romantic comedy classics like *You've Got Mail, Sleepless in Seattle,* and *When Harry Met Sally,* you owe her one, too.

She made you laugh, she made you cry, but Ephron wasn't just a funny face. Armed with her sharp wit, she broke through the ranks in Hollywood and was an outspoken critic of the wage gap and the male-dominated workforce. Through her writing and films, she brought honest explorations of male and female dynamics into mainstream media in an understated, humorous way.

I TRY to WRITE PARTS for women THAT are AS COMPLICATED and INTERESTING as WOMEN ACTUALLY ARE.

I HAD REASONED this OUT in my MIND; THERE WAS one OF two THINGS I HAD a RIGHT to, LIBERTY or DEATH; IF I COULD NOT HAVE one, I WOULD HAVE the other.

HaRRieT TuBMaN

(1822–1913)

THROUGHOUT HISTORY, there have been few as selflessly heroic as Harriet Tubman.

It is one thing to risk your life to escape from slavery, which she did in 1849. It is quite another to risk death perhaps hundreds of times in order to save others. Though the exact number of slaves she rescued is unknown, Tubman earned the nickname Moses for her role leading slaves to freedom as a "conductor" in the Underground Railroad for a reason. Her intelligence and courage also aided her as a scout, a spy, and a nurse during the Civil War.

Tubman continued showing up and stepping up long after the war. She rallied for women's right to vote and dignity for black women, and used the proceeds from her speeches to fund the Home for Aged and Indigent Negroes, which she built in her own residence.

PaTTi SMiTH

(1946–PRESENT)

IN A notoriously male arena of pop culture, Patti Smith is a rock star among rock stars.

A piercingly honest writer, Smith is known for her emotionally raw lyrics and crafty wordplay. She began her trailblazing career with poetry readings and went on to publish several collections of her poems, all while writing about music as a journalist for magazines such as *Rolling Stone.*

By setting her poetry to music, she became a pioneer of punk rock. Her first album, *Horses,* is a 1970s New York punk rock classic, and still makes the top 100 of virtually every "best albums of all time" list. It's hard to look at music of the last forty years and not see Smith's influence.

Smith has always stood out from the predominantly male rock landscape, pushing new boundaries for feminism, individuality, and musical expression.

WE GO THROUGH *Life.*
WE SHED OUR SKINS.
WE BECOME *ourselves.*

We HAVE to BUILD THINGS that WE WANT to SEE ACCOMPLISHED, IN *Life* AND IN *our* COUNTRY...

to MAKE SURE THAT OTHERS...

DO NOT *have* TO SUFFER

the SAME DISCRIMINATION.

Patsy Mink

(1927–2002)

BREAKING DOWN gender inequalities in education and taking names, Patsy Mink wasn't afraid of the word *no*. And that's a good thing, because she heard it a lot.

Facing racial discrimination as an undergraduate, she organized with students, faculty, and businesses to force the University of Nebraska to desegregate its student housing. After twenty different medical schools turned her down due to gender discrimination, she attended law school instead. She became the first woman to open a private law practice in the state of Hawaii, served in the Hawaii State Senate, then became the first woman of an ethnic minority to be elected to the U.S. Congress.

During her time in Congress (six consecutive terms), she passed landmark legislation for equality in education, both for young children and for women in higher education. We see what you did there, Patsy.

THE *more* CLEARLY WE CAN FOCUS *our* ATTENTION ON THE *wonders* AND REALITIES *of* THE UNIVERSE ABOUT US, the LESS *taste* WE SHALL *have* FOR DESTRUCTION.

RacHeL CarSon

(1907–1964)

RACHEL CARSON was a crusader for environmental truth.

Carson's educational background was in marine biology, and her research as a natural scientist in search of truth led her to publish articles, write books, and deliver speeches on her findings—all with the goal of raising greater public awareness and understanding of the environment. She gained so much attention with her early work that, even though it was against her wishes, an Academy Award–winning documentary was created about her discoveries.

Later in her career, Carson directed her work toward environmental conservation. She was one of the first people to speak out on the controversial subject of pesticides, penning the bestselling *Silent Spring* to document the harmful effects that pesticides had on the environment. Her work challenged the chemical companies and inspired a movement that eventually led to the creation of the Environmental Protection Agency.

My MOTHER told me TO BE A *Lady*. AND for HER, THAT MEANT BE *your* OWN PERSON, BE INDEPENDENT.

RUTH BADER GINSBURG

(1933–PRESENT)

IN THE sport of law, Ruth Bader Ginsburg has played her best game straight from the bench.

Ginsburg enrolled at Harvard Law School in 1956, one year after giving birth to her daughter. Reportedly, the dean asked her and her fellow female students how they felt about taking spots from qualified men. Perhaps this fueled the fire with which she fought gender discrimination over her long legal career, especially as general counsel for the ACLU.

She is the second woman ever to serve on the U.S. Supreme Court. Though her list of legal accolades is long, she is best known for being one of America's greatest legal advocates for gender equality. Her rulings on cases dealing with wages, suffrage, abortion, and birth control have made land-mark strides for women's rights. And Ginsburg's advocacy has not stopped at gender equality—throughout her tenure, she has crusaded for equal rights for all. In 2013, she became the first Supreme Court justice to officiate a same-sex marriage ceremony.

In more casual circles, she is lovingly referred to as the Notorious RBG.

OPRAH WINFREY

(1954–PRESENT)

SHE'S BEEN called the world's most powerful woman, the greatest black philanthropist in American history, and the queen of all media. Check, check, check.

Oprah Winfrey's impressive rise from rags to riches is not so much a "lucky break" story as it is a testament to hard work, owning her natural charisma, and a knack for doing business with integrity. She landed a radio job while in high school and began anchoring the local news while she was still a teen. From there, she took over a local Chicago daytime TV talk show, which eventually became the *Oprah Winfrey Show*, and gained popularity at a tremendous rate, going on to launch her own production company.

Winfrey became an international sensation, even embarking on a successful acting career while building her media empire. Her decision to use her platform to explore topics centered on self-care and soulful living, as opposed to the common TV trash talk, has helped her create a lasting level of influence and loyalty among her audiences.

As the first African American billionaire, Winfrey has focused on giving back in big ways, such as opening a girls' school in South Africa and donating to rebuilding efforts after Hurricane Katrina. In terms of Oprah's generous "giveaways," her education efforts may be the most meaningful: *You* get an education! *You* get an education! And *you* get an education!

Making A **BOLD** MOVE IS the ONLY *way* to ADVANCE TOWARD *the* GRANDEST **VISION** *the* UNIVERSE HAS *for* YOU.

One IS NOT BORN, BUT RATHER Becomes, A WOMAN.

SiMONe de Beauvoir

(1908–1986)

FROM MARCHES and speeches to bra burnings and picket lines, women have pushed for equality of the sexes in many different ways.

Few, though, have examined feminism in such thoughtful and existential terms as Simone de Beauvoir. De Beauvoir was many things: a writer, an intellectual, a political activist, and a philosopher—but above all, she was a feminist.

Her 1949 philosophical treatise, *The Second Sex*, is an in-depth examination of the oppression and liberation of women. It is regarded as a seminal work of feminist theory that deeply influenced the second wave of feminism. She went on to write many other revolutionary works of philosophy and fiction, ultimately winning the Prix Goncourt, France's highest literary prize.

De Beauvoir, who had a lifelong open relationship with philosopher Jean-Paul Sartre, played a big role in France's women's liberation movement in the 1970s. Her feminist teachings have inspired generations and still live on today.

SOPHIE SCHOLL

(1921–1943)

IS THERE anything you believe in so much that you'd die for it?

Sophie Scholl was a German student who was active in a nonviolent, anti-Nazi group called the White Rose. She helped author and distribute a series of pamphlets that instructed Germans on how to peacefully resist the Nazi government. These pamphlets were secretly circulated throughout Germany by six core members of the White Rose, including Scholl's own brother, during the summer of 1942.

Scholl and the rest of the group's members were arrested, found guilty of treason, and sentenced to death in February 1943. She was just twenty-one years old.

In her short life, Scholl lived courageously and passionately—and she died full of certainty that her actions would speak louder than the Nazis' hate.

Take CARE HOW you PLACE your MOCCASINS upon THE *Earth,* STEP with CARE, FOR the FACES of THE FUTURE *generations* ARE LOOKING UP *from* THE *Earth,* WAITING THEIR TURN *for* LIFE.

WiLMa MaNKiLLeR

(1945–2010)

IN THE storm that is life, Wilma Mankiller stood like a tree.

A community organizer and Native American activist, she was the first woman to serve as chief of the Cherokee Nation. Conquering gender stereotypes as well as two serious diseases and a nearly fatal automobile collision, Mankiller was a survivor in both her professional and personal life. She embodied the sense of tenacity reflected in the Cherokee people and strengthened their economy and tribal government, investing those gains in health care, education, housing, and job training.

Instead of waiting around for others to create a better world for the Cherokee people, Mankiller enacted the change herself. In 1998, she received the Presidential Medal of Freedom.

GRACE JONES

(1948–PRESENT)

PERHAPS TO some, "sex symbol" is a derogatory title that distracts from the ideals of feminism. But not when it's the 1980s, your name is Grace Jones, and you're busy redefining beauty standards and breaking through stereotypes as quickly as one can say "vogue."

Singer, songwriter, supermodel, and so much more, the Jamaican-born Jones is known for her distinct androgynous features, her unique take on new wave music, and, of course, her "don't give a damn" attitude toward her critics and haters.

As a thin and timid child, it would have been hard to guess that that little girl would one day blossom into the powerhouse of unabashed self-expression for which she is now known. At seventeen, she decided to leave college for Paris to pursue a modeling career. She placed a bet on her unconventional look and won. Top names in the fashion world took notice. From there, she launched into the music world, becoming a prolific figure in the 1980s nightclub scene. She would go on to reinvent herself yet again with her acting career, starring in films such as *A View to a Kill*, part of the James Bond series.

To any of the critics who told her it couldn't be done: Move along, darlings.

Yayoi Kusama

(1929–PRESENT)

WITH MENTAL illness as her muse, Yayoi Kusama has broken the rules for more than fifty years, redefining the artistic canvas and inspiring other artists to do the same.

When she was a child, Kusama started having hallucinations that she then channeled into her drawings. She grew up in a family that condemned her creativity, so she left home to pursue her art free of confines. She moved to New York City and created highly immersive and often controversial exhibits (including some in which she painted polka dots on nude men and women) before being committed to a mental institution in Tokyo, where she voluntarily lives and works to this day.

Her art has shaped the work of widely recognized artists, from pop icon Andy Warhol to minimalists such as Donald Judd. For Kusama, art is life, and her unique perspective (and her colorful bobbed wigs) continue to delight and inspire.

I WANTED to START A Revolution, USING ART TO BUILD the SORT of SOCIETY I myself ENVISIONED.

ZaHa HaDiD

(1950–2016)

THE PHRASE "think outside the box" might be a metaphorical cliché, but when it came to abstract architectural thinking, Zaha Hadid decided "there are 360 degrees, so why stick to one?" An Iraqi British architect, she is known for her unique structures that "liberated architectural geometry," according to the *New York Times*, and she is referred to by the *Guardian* as the "queen of the curve."

Looking at her work, you can see why. Some of her most notable "deconstructivist" designs include the London Aquatics Centre built for the 2012 Olympics, Michigan State University's Eli and Edythe Broad Art Museum, and the MAXXI National Museum of 21st Century Arts in Rome. The talented architect racked up accolades that had not been won by women previously, such as the Pritzker Architecture Prize and the London Design Museum's Design of the Year Award.

Though she has since died, many of Hadid's buildings are still under construction, foreshadowing that some of her best work is yet to come.

IF I were A GUY,

WOULD THEY CALL me A Diva?

TRUE PEACE IS NOT *merely* the ABSENCE OF WAR; IT IS *the* PRESENCE *of* JUSTICE.

Jane Addams

(1860–1935)

MEET THE mother of social work.

In a society where the role of the family matriarch was limited to tending house and raising children, Jane Addams chose instead to mother an entire nation by advancing local public health, improving the lives of children, and promoting international peace efforts.

Addams spent her entire life dedicated to helping those less fortunate than her. Social settlements didn't really exist at that time in the United States, and Addams decided that they should. She kick-started her career in service to the underprivileged when she established the Hull House in Chicago, a settlement home to help newly arrived European immigrants, and later expanded to welcome diverse communities, including Mexicans and African Americans. A prominent speaker and advocate for education, she gave lectures all over the country to those who could not afford a formal education by meeting the people where they were. Ahem . . . the original TED Talks? Her teachings and written works resulted in a movement that pushed for social justice, pacifism, and gender equality and influenced national reform.

It should come as no surprise that Addams went on to become the first American woman to win the Nobel Peace Prize.

GLORIA STEINEM

(1934–PRESENT)

BOTH DEEPLY admired and disliked, Gloria Steinem didn't become one of the most well-known feminist activists of our time by being polite or keeping quiet.

Since the 1960s, she has written passionately about controversial subjects such as same-sex marriage, contraception, abortion, and career-versus-marriage and spoken out with a fervor that has propelled her to political influence and popularity. She cofounded *Ms.* magazine in 1972 because she "realized as a journalist there was really nothing to read that was controlled by women."

Steinem has been showing up for more than fifty years to bring women's and human rights to the forefront of our culture's conversation. Her longevity as a pillar of feminism is due not only to her brains and determination but also to her commitment to intersectionality as the key to the women's movement.

Most recently, at the age of eighty-two, she cochaired and spoke at the 2017 Women's March on Washington.

CORETTA SCOTT KING

(1927–2006)

THE WORLD needs more love. And that's just what Coretta Scott King brought to it.

King was an activist who took part in the Montgomery bus boycott and helped pass the Civil Rights Act. You might know her as the wife of Martin Luther King Jr., but after her husband's assassination, she continued to spread her message of love, acceptance, and freedom for those who were being denied basic rights. Traveling the world, she lectured on a variety of issues, from environmental justice to the needs of the poor, homeless, and marginalized.

Above all, King did not believe in speaking out for freedom for one group of people while denying it to others. She lived her life standing up for those who couldn't stand up for themselves, regardless of race, age, gender, or religion.

Women, IF THE SOUL of THE NATION is to BE SAVED, I Believe THAT YOU MUST BECOME ITS Soul.

Profile an influential woman from your own life here:

ACKNOWLEDGMENTS

IT IS with great appreciation that I give thanks to the special people who helped breathe life into this book. Your support has impacted my life in a significant, unforgettable way.

I'd like to express gratitude to the following in particular:

Cindy Uh: for sharing in this vision and your desire to illuminate these women and their stories with me.

Sarah Murphy, Hannah Robinson, and the team at Harper Wave: for your mutual excitement and belief in this book.

To Meg Ruggieri, Hannah Faust, Sarah Steiner, Megan Helseth, Dan Webster, Holly Hursley: for helping me ensure the integrity of the words and biographies.

To all my friends, family, and partner, Gregory: thank you for your enduring support, insight, and belief in me and in this project.

To my daughter, Luca, whom I'll welcome into the world this spring: you've made me realize my potential and power as a woman. You were my muse during this book's journey.

Finally, my utmost thanks to the women featured in this book. Your words and personalities are a constant source of inspiration, and I'm honored to have been given an opportunity to celebrate you.

KIMOTHY JOY is a Denver-based artist, social activist, and creative consultant whose signature style combines watercolor and ink pen with hand lettering. Her work appeared around the world following the 2017 Women's March on Washington, and she has since contributed art and collaborated with Melinda Gates, I Am That Girl, She's the First, Gucci, Juniper Books, author Jessica Bennett, and poets Nikita Gill and Cleo Wade. Her work has also been featured on media platforms such as the *Huffington Post*; *Teen Vogue*; *O, The Oprah Magazine*; Refinery29; *Glamour*; and many others.

Kimothy's artwork aims to add a sincere and hopeful message of empowerment to women in a conversation where it is often lacking. As a consultant, she has focused her efforts on national health care quality-improvement campaigns and has served an array of social organizations, including Smart Girl, Susan G. Komen, and the Soul Day Foundation. In addition, she has organized and participated in Denver's TEDx programs to help incite change and spread progressive ideas.